The Debt-Free Plan

How to Become Debt-Free

by Christopher R. Hofbauer

ISBN: 978-0-578-72001-2

Table of Contents

The Debt-Free Plan

My Journey to Becoming Debt-Free

Living a life with debt can be overwhelming. You may feel suffocated and become frustrated when trying to get it under control. If these struggles are not addressed, your physical and mental health will be negatively affected. Overcoming these struggles is no easy task; however, the road to becoming debt-free will be a major learning experience and an opportunity for personal growth. The debt I had accumulated eventually became one of the greatest things that could have happened to me. It put me in a survival mindset, forced me to learn how to navigate through life with debt, and forced me to learn the necessities of financial planning. The tools and skills I learned from my journey in becoming debt-free have been instrumental in other successes I have achieved in my life. The topics here are practices, procedures, and guidelines that helped me overcome my debts. My hope is that they do the same for you and that you will use the material in this book as a guide to get you through your journey. You can also visit www.thedebtfreeme.com to take the financial assessment and easily access all the tools that will be covered in the book.

The events that transpire in your life define you and tell the story of who you are today. How you ended up in your current position is a consequence of the decisions you made and the outcomes of those decisions. Your debts did not magically appear; taking them on was a choice you made and one that you must accept as a reality. Eliminating your debts is a choice you need to make as well. There are no shortcuts in this process. The road to achieving financial freedom is long and tedious, and you must be diligent in your approach. If there is one takeaway from these lessons, let it be that consistency and sustainability are the keys to accomplishing any goals in life. Overcoming debt is no exception.

Graduating from college brought me feelings of fear, depression, and anxiety over the five years of student loan debt I accumulated. My family did not have an abundant college fund in place to pay for my education. I certainly wanted to be successful and to be able to make a decent living for myself and my future family. Therefore, the only way I would be able to go to college to get a degree was by taking out student loans. Carrying the burden of student loan debt was only a small price to pay for the opportunities that getting a degree has provided.

Through my time in college, I paid no attention to the amount of student loan debt I was accumulating. The amount of interest that would accrue or the total amount of money that would be due each month after graduation had been an afterthought. I did not truly comprehend all of these aspects of the debt I was acquiring. As graduation neared, it was evident that my debt total would be high. Admittedly, at this time I still did not fully understand what that truly meant. While approaching graduation, I put together a spreadsheet with the total amount of debt I had acquired. It was overwhelming to see the total amount that I owed and had to begin repaying. My world was turned upside down and I felt sick when I saw that the amount of debt totaled $134,617. Once I landed a job after graduation, finally earning money had me feeling on top of the world, at least for a period of time. Negative thoughts and depression ensued with the realization that I had to repay a debt of this magnitude. My knowledge of finances was limited at the time; I graduated with a technology degree and did not take any personal finances classes as a student, but I knew I needed to develop a strategy to pay my debts off as quickly as possible.

I was going to have to be disciplined, and it would be a grind to pay down this mountain of debt. I would have to make sacrifices and live a lifestyle that would give me the greatest chance to successfully achieve my goals. I took action and gained a strong grasp on my financial situation, clearly defined my goals, and developed a well thought out strategy on the approach I was going to take in paying off my debt. This process was the foundation to my success. Lacking in any one of these areas would have decreased the likelihood of success.

The journey will test your patience as it did mine, and it will require discipline. As soon as you accept this realization, you will be able to move on to building an approach that will allow you to successfully reach your goals. While the decision to be disciplined is easy, the actual practice to be disciplined is not. The truth is that it will take time to become debt-free. During my journey, I had thoughts of giving up on my aggressive timeline and to switch to paying only the minimum amount due on my debts. However, I knew that if I were to abandon my plan and strategy, I would be paying my debt for years past the date I had set as my goal. Reflecting on my situation and determining my reason for wanting my debts gone became a powerful tool. In addition, I had to make sure my lifestyle was sustainable in order to be successful in sticking to my strategy.

Strong discipline will require you to have a level of control over your mindset. This ability to properly control your thoughts and emotions is critical in guiding you through this journey. Over the years, I utilized each of these methods and approaches to maintain control over my mindset. To this day, they continue to benefit my life and help me to be successful in accomplishing my goals.

Chapter Exercises

1. How quickly would you like to pay off your debt?

_____

_____

_____

2. Describe your financial knowledge:

_____

_____

_____

3. How confident are you in paying off your debt?

_____

_____

_____

_____

Mindset

Your mindset is an important component to everything you do in life. Your thoughts can become your reality. When you have negative thoughts, you tend to draw negativity into your life. This is true with debt as well. If you take a look at your debt and think "I will never pay my debt off" or "This is going to take forever," then those thoughts can become reality. With this negative mindset, you will likely struggle to pay down your debt, or worse, your debt's total may increase due to missed payments or not paying down the interest causing the debt to balloon leaving your debt exponentially more than you had borrowed. Instead, have a positive mindset and outlook on debt. A positive mindset will not only make you happier, but will also attract and draw positivity into your life. Thinking positively is certainly not easy; it takes practice, time, and constant correction, especially when it comes to debt. Debt can be daunting, smothering, and a major burden on your life. Start by replacing the negative thoughts of "I will never pay off my debt" or "This is going to take forever" with the more positive "My debt is going to be paid off before I know it."

  I felt overwhelmed, anxious, and depressed with the total amount of debt that I owed. $134,617 was on my mind all day, every day. It consumed my thoughts and made me sick. I questioned how I got myself into this situation. I blamed my debt on everyone and everything except myself. I reflected on this way of thinking and knew it was not healthy. My mindset needed to change if I wanted to get ahead of this debt. I had accepted these loans, and they were my responsibility. I had to find my own way out of this situation. After reading how others had paid off their debts, I realized that my mentality would be everything. To become debt-free, the first step would be to change my current mindset and shift my focus to positivity and taking my debt seriously.

The most significant shift in my mindset began when I started to ask myself what things in life were the most important to me and if my debt was causing any stress or separating me from them in any way. Once I was able to answer this question, I had the motivation I needed, and I was able to prioritize my debt. My first step was to write down everything that was or would be affected by having debt. I reviewed this list, and every item would improve if I were able to live a lifestyle free of financial burden.

Take time to think about the aspects of your life that mean the most to you. Reflect on these and what they mean to you. Then think about your debt and how it is affecting each one of them. Envision how these aspects of your life would improve if you did not have debt. Not having debt gives you a sense of freedom and happiness that will radiate throughout all areas of your life. Gaining a true understanding of what is most important to you may not come as easy to some as it does for others. However, there are tools that we will cover that can help to get you to that place, and it all starts with feeling grateful for your current position.

Having a feeling of gratitude for your current position in life is extremely important for your well-being. Feelings of gratitude reflect outward in your life; therefore, it is important that you feel grateful for whatever position you are in. Your situation could always be worse, and no matter how bad you think you have it in life, there is always someone who has it worse. How you see the world has a major impact on the direction of your life. Throughout my journey, I have found a few mental exercises that have helped strengthen my mindset and helped to maintain a strong feeling of gratitude toward my past, my current position, and the future of my life. These exercises included meditation, journaling, physical activity, cold shock therapy, and breathing exercises. Each of these mental exercises has helped me at different stages of my journey. I do not do all of these exercises every day; I experiment and find the one (or more) that is most effective at the time. Try each of these and find what works for you.

Meditation is a technique that can be life changing. Meditation can help to soothe the mind, detach yourself from your outside world, control your thoughts, and give you a chance to reset your current mindset. There are many ways to practice meditation, but the most common is the use of a mantra. Creating a mantra is a simple process. Start by developing a phrase or series of words that carry weight and have a powerful meaning to you. Once you have your mantra, go into a dark and silent room, get comfortable, set a timer, close your eyes, and continuously repeat your mantra until the time is up. This form of mediation can be done at any time of the day. Doing this in the morning can set a tone for the day. Whereas at night, it tends to refresh the individual and reset them after a long day. After these sessions, my mind feels clear and I am focused on my goals. Meditation requires a level of patience and the ability to stay calm to let yourself fall into a meditative state. If meditation is not for you, there are other approaches to strengthening your mindset.

Journaling is a highly effective technique to get thoughts out of your head and adjust your mindset. There are many approaches to journaling. One approach is to write down three to five things every morning that you are grateful for. This approach starts the day off with positivity, which will bring positivity to other areas of your life. Another approach is to write down the things you want to accomplish each day, then revisit them at the end of the day. At this point, you will observe what you have accomplished, and review what prevented you from accomplishing what you did not.

An alternative approach is to write about anything and everything that comes to mind. I typically begin by describing how I feel at that moment: I write about the things that bother me, the things I am happy about, and anything else that crosses my mind. I find it beneficial to write whatever thoughts come to mind first. Once you begin to write and flow with your thoughts, you will begin to express your true feelings toward your life and your current situation. You can later revisit these journal entries and reflect on what you have written. Take time to reflect on any negativity you may write about, and think about how much it truly matters. I have found this process to be therapeutic. Otherwise, I would have all these thoughts and feelings in my head that I did not know how to express. I bottled them up, and it began to eat at me. Your thoughts define who you are. They become your feelings, and feelings become actions. When your mind is weak, the tension and stress will begin to build. The combination of tension and stress will eventually lead to negativity. This state of mind is counteractive for being disciplined and strong-willed in life.

Exercise is a tool to strengthen the mind as well. Exercising does not exclusively involve going to the gym or going for a run. While these are very effective at reaching a level of mental clarity, these are not the only methods. Simply going for a walk can be extremely beneficial. It can be therapeutic to walk and let your mind wander. For me, it is as simple as that. I sometimes wake up, dust off the cobwebs, and hit the streets. I walk around the block, just a short five-minute walk, before I start my day. These five minutes a day can have a major impact on the rest of the day. During these walks, there are many different things you can be doing to prepare your mind. Similar to the meditation approach, you can repeat your mantra as you walk to shift your focus and recenter yourself. You can also try thinking about everything on your mind, aside from your tasks for the day. Brain-dump during the walk and get all those thoughts out. When you focus your mind toward the tasks for the day, you can easily become overwhelmed and stressed. Getting in touch with your surroundings can be a powerful mental exercise during these walks. During walks, divert your attention and focus intently on all the things that are happening around you. Feel the sun on your skin, feel the wind in the air, hear the birds in the area, listen to the tires, exhaust, and engine from the cars driving by, and concentrate on all the smells in the air. As you embrace each of these, smile, and appreciate that you are capable of experiencing all of this. Doing this gives me gratitude for my environment. I wake up excited for my walks, and at the end of my five minutes, I am smiling, happy, and ready for the day ahead.

Cold shock therapy is another great tool for your physical and mental well-being. It is important to use caution when performing cold shock therapy and to consult with your physician before practicing these techniques. A traditional cold therapy treatment would be to fill a tub with ice, set a timer for one to five minutes, and sit in the tub until the timer ends. Another, and less involved, approach would be to take a cold shower. Under these extreme conditions, the body and mind are forced to overcome the cold temperature. During this process your body will go into a survival state, and the shock to your system can make you feel better and help to sharpen the mind. This mental exercise is perfect for those who need help practicing their discipline. By bracing against the cold for a few minutes without giving in, you have overcome your mind's flight signals, and have increased your ability to stay disciplined. During these cold treatments you will want to give up. The thoughts of it being too cold, or that you have been there long enough, will begin to creep into your mind. Do your best to fight the feeling of wanting to get out, and stay for the predetermined length of time. Once you are finished, you will feel amazing and focused. Under the extreme cold, your mind will be focused on the cold, and while your focus is on the cold, you will have relief from the thoughts that were previously on your mind. You will momentarily forget about the things that need to be completed at home or at work, the overwhelming commitments, bills, or your debt. Although this bit of clarity and simplistic thinking will only last a few minutes, the impact that it has on your mental state is phenomenal. Excessive thoughts that are not managed will begin to eat at you, and soon these manic thoughts will bleed into other areas of your life. They will begin to shape your actions and your relationships with people. It is crucial that you do not let your thoughts define you, and instead you define your thoughts. Any time you can remove yourself from these thoughts and shift your focus to something else, it is a successful moment. Getting through these cold sessions is not easy, the practice of a proper breathing technique is important here. Not only will proper breathing help to get you through these treatments, it will be beneficial in other situations of your life.

Proper breathing techniques are often overlooked as a valuable tool in managing stress. How you breathe can change your mental state as well as your physical state. You may come across situations that are stressful or that cause anxiety. Breathing through these will help ease the mind and re-align your focus. The journey of becoming debt-free is no exception. Debt can be overwhelming and a burden on your life. There will be times in your journey where you may revert back to negativity; you may feel bogged down and suffocated by your debt. It is important to not let those emotions control your life. When you have these feelings, proper breathing techniques can help turn things around as the focus shifts those previous thoughts to the breathing exercise.

A proper breathing technique is to take a deep breath and, while focusing on your breath, expand and draw the breath into your stomach, then into your chest, and continue until you reach your capacity. Repeat this process for a few minutes. Another breathing technique, commonly referred to as the "Box Breathing" technique or "four-square" breathing, is to take a four second inhale, hold the breath for four seconds, exhale for four seconds, then hold for four seconds, and repeat. Repeat this process three to five times. Once these exercises are completed, you will feel focused and relieved of stress.

These techniques can be used as a standalone mental exercise, or they can be combined to enhance other mental exercises and make them more effective. In meditation, you can replace your mantra with breathing patterns. In journaling, breathe through any mental blocks to get your thoughts rolling again. During walks, breathing can help you become more receptive to your surroundings. On my walks, I begin and end with a breathing exercise. Doing this prepares me for the start of the walk, and changes my mindset to win the day by the end of it. Breathing can also be extremely useful during cold therapy. Proper breathing techniques will help take your mind off the cold, and allow your body to overcome it. The breathing will help to center and reset the mind, which can be crucial for turning any negative and stressful thoughts into positive ones.

Negativity should be eliminated from your life as much as possible. Living a life with negativity is unhealthy and can bring about unnecessary stress. Feeling negatively toward your debt will not make your situation any better. Being faced with a mountain of debt is not an ideal situation for anyone. Feeling down on yourself and having regret will not pay off your debt any sooner. Embrace your debt and face it head on. When faced with debt, you will be forced to strengthen your mind, learn about finances, and work on your discipline. Due to my student loans, my understanding of personal finances strengthened and my appreciation for life grew. During the journey of paying off your debts, you will be faced with challenges. With a strong mindset, you will be able to overcome these challenges and successfully progress through your journey and become debt-free.

Adjusting your mindset to positivity will be challenging. Accomplishing this requires practice. Returning to your mental exercises will be instrumental in achieving a positive mindset. Letting the negativity take over is easier, as it becomes a way to divert ownership of the situation and place blame. It provides an escape by removing any of your responsibility and focusing instead on external factors. Replace these thoughts with positive ones, even if you do not truly believe them yet. Believing these thoughts is not important during the beginning stages. Continue to think positively and eventually you will begin to believe it. Tell yourself your debt will be paid off soon, that you make plenty of money to pay down your debts, and that you can continue to make payments, regardless of your situation. You will begin making better choices regarding your finances with this mental shift. You will feel better knowing you actually can be strong-willed and disciplined. Once your debt is paid off, you will end your journey with a skillset and discipline that you did not have before. It all starts with a shift in mindset.

Doing the same mental exercises over time may eventually become stale; you might begin to lose interest, or they may begin to be not as effective as they once were. Keep these mental exercises fresh. Use different techniques at different times as well as changing variations of the routines themselves. My routine evolved and changed throughout my entire journey. In the early stages, going for walks and runs helped to clear my mind. These sessions helped to get my mindset in the right place and put my situation into perspective. This allowed me to develop a strategy that best suited my ability to pay my debt off as quickly as possible. Eventually, putting my strategy in place became stressful, and the stress did not fade during my walks or runs anymore. Instead, I would have racing thoughts about my strategy. To combat this stress, I turned to journaling. I recognized that the stress that was building up was due to the constant, inescapable thoughts on my strategy. Through journaling, I was able to get these thoughts out of my head and onto paper.

After a while of consistently making payments, I began to get complacent. I had made a major dent in my debt but I could not escape the feeling that I had spent thousands of dollars and still had so far to go. The idea of abandoning my strategy and to begin paying less into my debt began to creep into my thoughts. I knew that with this negative mindset, I would not reach my goals, and I did not want this to happen. To correct my mindset, I started to practice meditation and breathing techniques. Meditation helped to reset my focus to being goal oriented, and my attitude shifted to what I had believed was most important. Combining meditation with breathing exercises kept this mindset in place. The *why* in my life was revived, and whenever doubts would arise, I took a second to myself, visualized life with my goals completed, and re-centered.

Visualization is a powerful tool to strengthen your mindset. The power of visualization is often understated. The greatest athletes and businessmen and women in the world all have a great vision of themselves and what they want to achieve. You may imagine being in certain situations or achieving particular outcomes, such as scoring a game winning goal or closing a major deal at work. However, true visualization needs to be practiced. It is the practice of knowing and believing exactly what and where you want to be, imagining those thoughts with great detail, and not losing sight of them. How you will get there does not matter at this point, but rather your belief and desire that makes all the difference.

Your thoughts become your reality. Focus your thoughts on success, hard work, and discipline. Being debt-free is not always the easiest to visualize. You are constantly reminded of your debts, and with interest accumulating, it can feel that there is no end in sight. Visualization can be extremely useful when applied to debt. Tell yourself, *I **will** pay my loans down. It will take time and a lot of effort, but they **will** be paid down.* Take time to really think about how life will be without debt. Visualize where you will be at the exact time you pay your debt off, and who will be with you as you submit that final payment. Repeatedly visualize this moment and see it with great detail. Throughout my journey, I would begin to feel depressed about my loan totals and my timeline. Whenever these negative thoughts occurred, I would take a second to close my eyes and visualize making my last payment. I would focus on how that moment was going to feel. I would begin to smile like the moment was happening, and think about the journey that I just endured. In those moments, I truly believed that I was capable of achieving my goals. This process may seem trivial;

however, when that moment finally came, it was everything I had visualized. My vision became reality.

Dedication can be a key attribute that will help you get through this journey. Great accomplishments are the product of hard work, discipline, and dedication. Dedication is healthy when directed toward the right things. Being dedicated helps you stay focused, and is necessary in order to achieve great accomplishments. Dedication is also a key driving factor for long-term motivation. The beginning of a journey is often filled with excitement and desire. Over time, that excitement and desire can begin to wane. This is the case whether it be a new diet, school, or paying down debt. In these instances, having a level of dedication can be healthy and lead to an attitude that will ensure you stay focused on your goals. Having this internal drive only becomes unhealthy when it begins to degrade your health or your relationships. Otherwise, not only is it healthy to be dedicated, but it is necessary in many cases.

With dedication you will have a goal-oriented mindset, and with your focus being on your debt, you will be able to make proper decisions. You may often be faced with the dilemma of spending money on something that you want, rather than what you actually need. You will begin to convince yourself that you need these things and that you should just go ahead and buy them. Instead of impulsively making purchases, with the proper dedication toward your debt you will be able to focus on what is truly necessary rather than items that will push you further from your goals. I was constantly battling the desire to make unnecessary purchases throughout my journey to become debt-free. However, I was dedicated to becoming debt-free, and that meant more to me than whatever I was considering buying. It is important to return to what matters most and make the correct decision. True dedication fosters discipline, and discipline is the key to accomplishing any of your goals.

Discipline is the most significant attribute when it comes to achieving anything in life. It is a constant battle every day. Your discipline is similar to a muscle in that the more you work it, the stronger it becomes. However, like exercise, it is imperative that you occasionally rest your discipline in order to avoid getting burnt out. It is common to have a lapse in discipline at times, but the likelihood of these occurring increases when you are strict for too long without any breaks. The odds of having a large swing toward becoming careless increases the longer you are disciplined. It is important to let go of the reins from time-to-time. When you are strict with every dollar you spend for a week or so, treat yourself to something small. You do not want to continue to be strict and then completely fall off the rails. You need to find a way to be sustainable in your journey. Including these small rewards can still be part of a structured plan, but be sure these breaks in discipline are short-lived. Discipline is too important to be completely abandoned.

Discipline is an essential element to achieve your goals. Become obsessed with your discipline, take pride in it, and have the mindset that you are disciplined. Even if you have no discipline yet and you are working on it, tell yourself that you are disciplined and that you have the mental fortitude to stay strong. Appreciate every opportunity life throws at you to strengthen your discipline. Every time you decide not to make an unnecessary purchase, your discipline grows stronger, and you should feel proud knowing that you have control. Gain control over your life: one step at a time, one mental exercise at a time, one opportunity at a time, one dollar at a time.

Now that your mindset is strong, you are ready to continue on the journey of becoming debt-free. You have determined what factors in your life are most important to you, and have gained control over your mind. You have developed practices to correct your mindset, and you are prepared to get after the next steps. The tools you have formulated will be monumental in the next stages. You now need to assess your finances so that you can redefine your objectives and begin setting goals on your way to success.

Chapter Exercises

1. What feelings do you have toward your debt?

_____

_____

_____

_____

_____

2. What are the most important things in your life? How does having debt affect these things?

_____

_____

_____

_____

_____

_____

3. What are you grateful for?

_____

_____

_____

_____

_____

4. What mental exercises did you try? Which of them has helped you? Describe how you felt before and after:

_____

_____

_____

_____

_____

_____

_____

5. Where will you be when you pay off your loans? Who will you be with?

_____

_____

_____

_____

_____

Financial Assessment and Strategy Building

Having a structured plan is a necessity. This part of the process is often overlooked, but doing so can inhibit your success. Without a structured plan and strategy, you are less likely to achieve your goals. It does not matter how strong your mindset is, how defined your goals are, or how passionate you are about becoming debt free; a plan makes it all come to fruition. For example, you can certainly build a house without a blueprint, but it will be a lot easier with one and fewer mistakes will be made along the way. Your plan will reveal what it will take to complete your goals, and it will give you the greatest opportunity for success.

It is important to start by taking a deep look into your finances and assess your current financial situation. It will be difficult to gauge how to properly set your budget without knowing everything about your finances. Make sure every dollar is accounted for when going through each of the upcoming steps. This process will also help to put your spending habits into perspective. Many would be surprised to learn the amount they actually spend on different items each month, let alone each week. When you dive deep into your finances and figure out where every dollar is going, you will begin to recognize any extraneous purchases. This allows you to be more strategic with your money, and put it towards your debt.

My first step was to make a spreadsheet to visualize my financial data (see an example of the completed spreadsheet at Appendix A. Visit www.thedebtfreeme.com to take the financial assessment and easily visualize your financial data). On the spreadsheet, I began dividing rows and columns into multiple categories: monthly income, fixed expenses, variable expenses, and debt. For each category, I made sure to be as specific as possible when entering my data. In the income category, I reviewed my paystub and entered the net income down to the penny. I did the same for my semi-monthly as well as my monthly totals (see completed income category in Appendix A). It is important to use your final "take home" pay, as this is the most accurate representation of how much money you actually have to put toward your expenses and debt each month. [1] Next are the fixed expenses; these are your bills that are the same cost every month. Leave no expenses behind; add everything regardless how

---

[1] If you contribute to a 401k, it will typically be taken from your Gross Income, and therefore, your Net Income will already include this expense.

low the cost. Every dollar needs to be accounted for so you can accurately set your budget.

Next, move on to the variable expenses. These are expenses that do not have a consistent amount each month and will vary based on usage. I found it difficult to get accurate values for these expenses without historic data. I reviewed all my previous credit card statements for the year, and searched for all commonly occurring expenses, such as: gas, groceries, restaurants, and entertainment. Using the credit card statements, I went through each of the last six months, calculated the totals of all these different expenses, and divided that number by six to get an estimate of the monthly average. Since these expenses are inconsistent, I decided to account for months where these expenses could be higher and I added 10% to these totals before entering these values into the variable expenses category. Living expenses could be split between the fixed and variable categories or placed in their own category. Structure these expenses in whichever way you find most beneficial. The majority of the living expenses will be fixed, such as rent or mortgage, internet, and cable. A few utilities such as electricity and water will be variable. Use the same approach that was taken when estimating other variable expenses. Calculate your average monthly usage, add 10% to this monthly average and use this value in your sheet. Adding this 10% buffer will help to ensure you will have enough money in your budget to put towards these expenses each month (an example of the fixed and variable expenses category can be found in Appendix A. For help assessing your finances visit: www.thedebtfreeme.com and take the financial assessment). The final step in assessing your finances is collecting and analyzing all debts.

Assessing your debt requires gathering some key metrics from the loan servicer. In this category on my spreadsheet, I listed each loan and included the following information for each: balance, interest rate, yearly cost, and amount due each month. Along with these details, I included the unique identifier of the loan to be used as a reference point in my strategy. In my case, each of my loans had a unique letter or a number (an example of these unique identifiers can be found in Appendix C). This unique identifier helps keep track of specific loans, which will be useful in your strategy to assure you are paying the right loan at each pay period.

Once all of the loan information has been gathered, it is time to build a concrete plan that maximizes your odds of success (see a completed debt overview in Appendix C. For help assessing your debts visit: www.thedebtfreeme.com). Gathering this data can be overwhelming, and since this can be one step in the journey that many dread, try to go into this with enthusiasm. If you can be enthusiastic about the process, there will be a greater chance you will stay disciplined and complete your plan. After all your debt information is listed, calculate the total of the minimum amounts due per month for each of the debt sources. Since this value is required to be paid each month, go back to your fixed expenses category, and create a new entry there with this value as **Total Debt Payment** (see the **Total Debt Payment** value within the Fixed Category in Appendix A). Do not worry about this value for now. You are only listing all your expenses, and this includes the minimum amount due on your debt that you are required to pay. Now that you have a grasp on your overall monthly expenditure, you can now determine your **Disposable Income** per month. To calculate your disposable income, subtract your total monthly expenses from your monthly **Net Income** (the formula to calculate for Disposable Income can be found in Appendix B). This disposable income represents the maximum amount that can be paid into your debt. I will later discuss approaches that can be taken to increase this value and reduce or eliminate unnecessary expenses.

In order to combat the dread of building my plan, I took a holistic approach into making this process bearable. I began with reflecting on how vital my mindset is when it comes to success. If you feel positive about your goals and get excited about planning them, your enthusiasm for the process will increase. You need to do everything in your power to develop this plan and strategy so that you can achieve them. Take a deep look at the first draft of your financial assessment and make sure you have everything listed. Make sure every dollar is accounted for, and any expenses that were inconsistent have a buffer built in to cover fluctuations.

Expanding on the debt category, calculate the current total balance of all of your loans, the average interest rate for all the loans, the yearly interest and monthly interest accumulated in dollars, and enter all of this data into a new section on the spreadsheet. To get the **Total Current Balance**, add each individual loan and enter the total in this field. The **Yearly Interest** can be calculated by adding all of the yearly interest for all loans and dividing that total by the total number of loans. For the **Average Interest Rate** field, multiply the total for all loans by the yearly interest. Next, to get the **Monthly Interest** divide the yearly interest value by 12. This information is vital to building a solid plan and formulating a strategy. It will be very useful when thinking about adding or removing expenses from the monthly budget. These cells in your spreadsheet must be calculated using formulas instead of fixed values (see these formulas in Appendix C). Using formulas will allow you to see how your additional debt payments will impact the overall timeline.

Seeing all of the debt in one place can be overwhelming. Especially when you see the total amount owed, and how much of that is from interest. Interest is the cost for borrowing money. When you agreed to borrow money from the bank for your loans, that original amount borrowed is considered the principle. The banks imposed a percentage rate that is applied to the principle, known as the interest rate. The principle multiplied by the interest rate is the amount of interest that will be added to the principle each year. Interest in particular can be especially frustrating, as this is money that continuously accumulates until the principal is paid in full. I found it beneficial to use interest as motivation. I worked harder and focused on paying as much as I possibly could into my debt in order to pay the least amount of interest over the term of the loans. In my case, if I were to pay the loans through the original term, I would have paid roughly $75,000 in interest. Instead, once I was finished paying down my debt, I had paid a total of $25,189.02. When you look at this on a savings basis, with the correct mindset, thorough planning, clearly defined goals, and staying disciplined with my strategy, I saved $50,000.

Once the expenses and debts are laid out, it is time to start to develop your strategy. There are a few extra sections to add to the spreadsheet that will help to develop your strategy. These are: **Months to Debt-Free** and **Debt-Free Date**. In order to get the **Months to Debt-Free** value, you could use the NPER formula in Excel or Google Sheets. In your spreadsheet, NPER will represent the number of months left until you are debt-free. The formula for this calculation is =NPER(average monthly interest rate, total monthly payment, total current balance). **Debt-Free Date** can be calculated by using the EDATE formula. This formula is =EDATE(current date, Months to Debt-Free) (an example of these formulas can be found in Appendix D. Calculators for **Months to Debt-Free** and **Debt-Free Date** can be found at www.thedebtfreeme.com). Having these in place will give you something to look forward to. It turns the thoughts of eventually paying off your debts into reality. Now that you can see there is an actual date on which you will be debt-free, you may be better able to visualize life at that time. Use that date to think about where you will be, what you will be doing at that time, and at what stages of life you will be in.

After you have your Months to Debt-Free and Debt-Free Date, create an **"Additional Payment"** category. Once the **"Additional Payment"** field is created, modify the **Total Monthly Payment** field to add the **"Additional Payment"** value to the sum (see an example of how to add the Additional Payment field into the Total Monthly Payment field can be found at Appendix F). Being tied into the monthly loan payment will show how this additional payment affects the timeline and interest accumulation. Those are the two values I chose to focus on, as it is motivating to see the date move closer, and the amount of interest decreases. Once everything was in front of me and I had a comprehensive view, I needed to figure out where to begin and build a solid strategy. I knew I had to be efficient with my money and leverage every dollar to maximize the additional payment and move the paid-off date as close as possible.

First, and most importantly, start by eliminating waste in your monthly expenses. This is a critical step in building a strategy that will enable you to be successful in achieving your goals. This step can be challenging. In order to make a drastic change in your life, you have to compromise. Extreme results are not achieved by doing the minimum. You need to completely change the way you think about money and your approach to spending it. Your focus and drive needs to be on your goals. The easiest place to begin is with fixed expenses. Review each expense in this category and determine which of these expenses you can get rid of, such as, memberships or subscriptions to services that do not get much use. Take a look at each expense and determine which of these you cannot live without, and which of them are unnecessary and are just nice to have. If a particular expense cannot be eliminated, explore all options to find a better price for it. Review plans for your cell phone, cable, internet, home and auto insurance, explore the area for gyms at reduced costs, etc. Make a phone call to the companies, and ask for a lower rate. Worst case scenario, they tell you no. Go over each of these expenses and explore all options to reduce cost.

Next, review the variable expenses. Try to find the cheapest options available for these common expenses as well. Go to the cheapest gas stations in the area when getting gas. When buying groceries, use coupons, find the store with the least expensive prices, purchase only what you need, and buy the cheapest options or alternatives for necessary items. You can be flexible with your purchases once your debt is eliminated, but while you are in debt-paying mode, you need to be cautious with spending. For variable expenses, it helps to set budgets and stick to them. You may find this to be easier to do with some expenses than it is with others. Personally, I did not want to eliminate going out to eat. Going out is an escape for me, and helped to keep me sane during my journey. Since I did not want to eliminate going out to eat, I instead decided to set a budget that would allow me to go out twice a month. I was able to stick to this budget throughout my journey and still achieve all of my goals.

Sticking to the budgets is not only about the money, but is also a mental exercise in discipline. If you are careless with your budget for one month, one month turns into two, two turns into three, and so on until you eventually start to miss your milestones and goals. The goals you set out to accomplish are sacred and must be protected, and budgets provide guidelines to assure that happens.

After some time, you will begin to see how eliminating unnecessary expenses impacts your finances. You can put any saved money toward your debt and see the direct impact this has on your timeline. If you are consistent, the overall impact over the course of paying into your debt will be monumental. For example, if you make daily stops for coffee, eliminating one coffee shop trip per week will save roughly $7/week, $28/month, and more than

$350/year. That one skipped coffee is an extra loan payment, and over time this will make a significant impact on your overall timeline.

The next phase in building a strategy involves taking a closer look at your debt. There are numerous strategies you can leverage in this process, such as: loan consolidation, modifying the terms of the loans, and repayment strategies.

Consolidation is a strategy that has multiple options, and there are pros and cons to each of these. Be careful if you are considering consolidating your debt. If you are not careful, it can cost you more money in the long run. In my case, I had loans that varied in interest rates from 3.4% to 7.9%. For the sake of convenience, I could have consolidated all my loans. However, if I were to lump all of the debt into one, I would have been given one term and one interest rate. All the debt that had lower interest rates would have been combined with the higher ones, and over time, I would have paid more in interest. If you are considering consolidation, make sure to pick and choose which loans you are combining, and only consolidate those which have similar interest rates. Another factor should be the time, or "life," left on the loan. If you are considerably closer to paying off a loan than you are to others, do not include that loan into your consolidation plan. Even if the interest rate is higher, it is better to leave that loan by itself. When shorter term loans are lumped with longer term loans, they all become one. You then lose the ability to pay off the shorter term loan quicker with the disposable income you have available.

You want to have the option to pay off debt earlier if possible.

In my case, I had 14 different student loans, each with their own balance, terms, and interest rates. I found it beneficial to leave these as individual loans since the interest rates and the "life" of the loans, or terms, varied too much for it to be beneficial to consolidate. The individuality allowed me to be flexible with my monthly payments. I was also able to be more effective with my **Additional Payment**, as I could target a specific loan based on my strategy. There are benefits to consolidation. For one, you will only have a single loan to focus on instead of multiples. Having multiple loans can be stressful to manage and may cause you to feel overwhelmed. Combining these loans into one can give you peace of mind and provide simplicity. The greatest benefit from consolidation can be the effect it has on your interest rates. When you combine all your loans, a new interest rate is applied to this new total. Any loans that had higher interest rates will now be subject to the new rate, which may be lower than your current rate.

This can be powerful if the majority of your debt is from high interest loans.

In continuing to review approaches to maximizing the efficiency in paying off your debt, modifying the term of the loans is another option which may have the largest impact on your timeline. If you have set a challenging timeline or are trying to pay down your debt as fast as possible, you need to be able to leverage every dollar. With this tactic in mind, it is beneficial to have the lowest possible minimum due for each loan per month. This allows you to strategically pay into the loans that will shorten your overall timeline the most. You must be careful when modifying the term of your loans. If you have a strong mindset and are disciplined, you will benefit from modifying the loan terms. I changed all of my loans to a 30-year plan, this lowered the minimum amount due each month. This in no way means that I intended to take my time and repay my loans over 30 years. Be cautious of this approach, the banks provide this offering because they collect more interest over time, and you do not want to fall into this trap. **Only do this if you can stay disciplined and execute your plan.** Extending the terms of your loans is a great tool to free up more money. This money can be used to target specific loans that will help move you closer to paying off your debts. For example, if you owed $300/month for ten years and then lengthen the loan term to a 30-year term, the payments would be roughly $160/month. This allows you to allocate nearly $140/month toward the principle of a higher-interest or higher-balance loan. In this approach, the total amount of debt owed does not decrease, but the total due each month does. This strategy can be frightening; 30 years is a long time, and you will not want to make payments for that long. You still need to pay the maximum amount possible toward your debt.

If you find changing the terms of your loans to be overwhelming and stressful, continue with the original term of the loans. Your mindset and attitude toward your goals are more important, and there are other approaches that can be used. At this stage in your strategy, you are ready to evaluate how you are going to choose which loans to pay first, and how quickly you are going to pay them. There are two main strategies for this, and choosing which one to go with has a lot to do with your mentality and what will help you stay on track. These methods include the Snowball and Avalanche plans.

The Snowball and Avalanche payment strategies are two of the most popular methods regarding the order in which to pay debt. In my approach, the Avalanche method involves paying each loan's minimum amount due per month, and then using any remaining funds from your budget to pay into the loan with the highest interest rate. In contrast, the Snowball method involves paying the minimum amounts due and then using any remaining budget to pay into the loan with the smallest balance. You begin to gain momentum as you pay off each balance. Once the smallest loan is paid in full, take the money that you were previously paying into that loan and now roll it into the next smallest balance.

The decision to choose the Snowball method or the Avalanche method comes down to your mentality and what will increase your likelihood of success. Traditionally, the Snowball method is known to inspire confidence. Targeting loans with the lowest balance first, means debt will be paid off sooner. This can act as motivation to help you stay on track toward your goals. The Avalanche method is directly focused on the **interest rates**, regardless of the balance. In this method, you will direct your additional payments towards the loan with the highest interest rate. Once that loan is paid in full, take the money you were previously paying into that loan and now roll it into the next loan with the highest interest rate. If the balance is also high on these loans, they will typically be the loans that are costing you more money in the long run. I like to think of interest as a bleeding wound and each payment toward higher interest loans slows the bleeding just a little. Comparing these methods in a mathematical perspective, the time it will take to pay down your debt will be nearly the same, unless you combine these and use a hybrid method.

Both the Snowball and Avalanche methods have their purposes, as they are both fundamentally powerful techniques to pay off debt. There are no wrong strategies, as long as you are disciplined and are paying into your debt, you will get to a $0 balance. When it came to my approach, I took a hybrid of the two methods. I chose to leverage both of these approaches at different times to achieve my goals and focused on the **monthly interest accumulated** for each loan. Interest can accumulate quickly and you want to minimize it as much as you can. In order to prioritize which loans you will be targeting, sort your debt in your spreadsheet by the amount of interest accumulated each month (see an example of how to sort your debt at Appendix E). As you continue to make payments, the amount of interest accumulated each month per loan will change. In the loans you are paying extra into, this value will decrease rapidly and will eventually be less than other loans. When this happens, re-sort your loans and shift your additional payments into the loan with the higher amount of interest accumulated each month. Continuing this process and sticking to this strategy will leave you paying less in interest over time.

Implementing a cadence for your payments is a powerful tool as well. Rather than paying into your debt on a monthly basis, make payments at a certain date or period of time. A popular and effective method is to pay into your debts on the day of your pay period. These payments would be a percentage of what you set as your budget for the month. For me, I get paid every two weeks and I would make a loan payment that was half of what I set for my monthly budget as soon as I received my paycheck. It will be more challenging to pay into debt the longer the money is in your bank account. When the money is in your bank account for a short amount of time, you feel less attached when it disappears. Having a healthy cadence can also help keep your goals in mind. You will see the impact you are having on your debt more frequently, and you will be excited that you are moving closer to your goals. Another major benefit to paying on an accelerated timeline, is the effect this has on the interest. With each payment your principal balance decreases, thus reducing the amount of interest that can accumulate. Smaller balance means less interest. Paying every one to two weeks will decrease the amount of interest you will end up paying over the course of the entire journey of becoming debt-free. In order to make sure you are staying on track and making your payments on schedule, set reminders. Create an event on your calendar for the date of your cadence, and set the reminder frequency according to your payroll schedule. If you are not currently using a calendar, get one. Reminders are useful tools; include them in your routine and use as many as you need so that you do not forget to make your payments.

In addition to the main spreadsheet, I created an additional sheet for the amortization of my debt. The amortization sheet represents the gradual reduction in the totals based on the amount being paid into the debt. This includes your additional payments and you will be able see the direct impact these have on your timeline. This sheet will be used to compose a timeline and to reference for motivation. The amounts and dates will be close estimates to what will transpire over the lifespan of the debt. To make the amortization schedule, use **Current Total Balance**, **Average Interest Rate**, and **Months to Debt-Free** from the debt category, current date, and **total monthly payment** from your expenses category. With this information, you will be able to build your amortization chart (see an example of a completed amortization chart at Appendix G; or, easily create an amortization chart at www.thedebtfreeme.com).

Having an amortization chart helped me to better define my goals and keep me focused as I was able to see where my loan balances would be at a given time in the future.

When entering the data, reference these values from your main spreadsheet, as this will show how the payments are affecting the timeline. To have the most accurate information in your spreadsheet, when you make a payment into any of your loans you will need to update the current total of that loan in your spreadsheet to reflect these changes. This is an important step as it will provide up-to-date information on the status of your debt. When you update your new totals with every payment, you will be able to return to the amortization chart and observe the impact.

There are no guarantees that this journey will go smoothly. I recommend adding an **Emergency Fund** category to account for any troubles along the way (an example of this category can be found at Appendix A). You should develop a backup plan that consists of having an adequate emergency fund to cover essential living expenses and your minimum payments due each month, for at least 2 to 6 months. Your backup plan may have an impact on how you execute your strategy. If you do not already have an emergency fund, you should allocate some, if not all, of your **Additional Payment** to this fund until you have an adequate amount saved.

Your planning is done, your strategy is in place, and you are now ready to define your goals. To stay focused, you built sections in the spreadsheets that show the number of months remaining and the date when all the debt will be paid off. This concrete strategy will promote a healthy mindset on the journey toward your goal to become debt-free. Throughout your journey, think about your payoff date, and picture the moment when you reach it. Envision where you will be and what life will be like. Those thoughts are powerful tools for motivation; use them to stay disciplined. Trust in your plan and do not let anything get in the way of it. Life happens, but do not abandon your plan. Instead, improvise, compromise, and adapt.

While creating these spreadsheets and calculations can be tedious, the tools provided will be extremely useful. Without these in place, it will be challenging to stay focused and disciplined, and you could be easily knocked off course. Use these tools to help keep you disciplined and to stick to your strategy, and you will be debt-free in no time at all.

Chapter Exercises

1. What are your fixed expenses? Which of these will you try to reduce or eliminate?

_____

_____

_____

_____

_____

2. What are your variable expenses? Which of these will you try to reduce or eliminate?

_____

_____

_____

_____

_____

3. After fixed and variable expenses, how much money can you put toward your debt?

4. Do you have an emergency fund? If so, how many months' worth of payments do you have saved to put toward your debt? The goal should be to have 2 to 6 months of payments saved. How do you plan to achieve this, and how long will it take you?

5. At what date will you have your debt paid off? Visualize this date and describe how you picture life at this time.

_____

_____

_____

_____

6. How frequently will you make payments? Have you set reminders for these payments?

_____

_____

_____

_____

_____

Goal Setting

When you have a desire to accomplish something in your life, goal setting is a critical step in order to be successful. Without having concrete goals, it is unlikely that you will achieve these desires. The important first step of the process should start with asking yourself, why? Each of your actions stem from a greater meaning or purpose. Not everyone will have the same *why*. When it comes to debt, the *why* could be as simple as: there is no other way out, you have to pay it back. Failure to pay the loans back can lead to damaged credit and wage deductions. Reflect on your mindset, and determine all your reasons why. No one else is responsible for your debt. Visualize the life you would like to be living. Now think about how debt has an effect on that life: your lifestyle, physical health, and mental state. Are you unable to take the trips you want to take? Are you unable to afford a nicer place or newer car? Debt will have a negative impact on your life. Use debt as motivation and develop structured goals that will help to guide you out of your current situation.

Now that you have reflected on your *why*, write it down and begin to break it down into a list of goals. For the moment, do not worry about how many goals you have. Throughout your life, your goals should be continuously growing and evolving. Just brain-dump and get everything written down. You will prioritize these later. Once the goals are written, they become real. You have the chance to look at them, evaluate them, and expand where needed. Keeping your goals in your head or written in your phone is not sufficient; you need to get them on paper. When you write your goals down on paper, the odds of accomplishing them increases. Now you are ready to further define these goals and format them in a way that will give you the greatest opportunity to be successful.

You want to be as specific as possible when you are creating your goals. Instead of writing down that you want to pay all debts, break them down further. Write that you want to pay off your student loans, credit card debt, car payment, etc. Then you want to break those down even further. If you have student loans from a co-signer, create separate goals for those co-signed loans. If you have more than one credit card, make a goal for each of those credit cards. These goals can then be broken down further, such as making a goal to pay certain student loans off by the end of the year, paying off a particular high interest loan, or a certain credit card.

Break down all of these goals into manageable chunks. Take a look at your goals, review each one, and create a series of milestones for the goal. Milestones should be actionable items that are the steps necessary to accomplish a goal. These milestones allow you to review your progress. This is important with any goal in life. My milestones were specific figures for my loans. Every $5,000 increment less on my overall debt was a milestone, as was every $50 less of accumulated interest per month. Achieving these milestones meant a lot to me. Some milestones may seem trivial and unnecessary, but the psychological and practical impact these have can be monumental. Every step closer to the goal is a major victory.

Goals that reference a timeline are important to have as well. A timeline helps track how you are progressing toward your overall goals. If you are continuously missing milestones, you will need to review your finances or reassess your strategy. Without a timeline, it can be difficult to stay disciplined and focused on your goals. However, putting a timeline on your goals can be challenging if you are not sure when you can achieve them. Be realistic and set an attainable timeframe based on your financial assessment. If you reach the end of the timeframe for that particular goal and you still do not have it crossed off the list, reassess, refocus, and then revise the goal's timeline. It is common for this process to happen frequently if you have set a challenging timeline. You may be tempted to be aggressive with your goals. If you fall short, you will need to positively reflect on your progress and take time to review how far you have come and how close you are to accomplishing your goals.

Now that you have a general idea of your goals, you need to begin to format them in a way that allows you to take action and work toward accomplishing them. The process of building concrete goals can be tedious and time consuming, but it is a critical step in this process and must not be overlooked. Up until now it did not matter if your goals were a bit messy; you have a general idea of what you want to accomplish and put them out on paper.

There are many ways to format goals, and there is no single approach that will work best for everyone. However, the following approach is what has been the most effective strategy for me throughout my life. It is commonly known as the **S.M.A.R.T.** method. This method implements a granular and methodical approach to goal setting. Using the **S.M.A.R.T.** method assists in thoroughly defining each goal, and brings to light aspects that may not have been considered previously. The acronym **S.M.A.R.T.** stands for: Specific, Measurable,

Attainable, Realistic, and Timely. These are key aspects in creating concrete goals, and when you are able to define each of these categories in detail, you will have well-defined goals.

Being Specific. You cannot have a general idea of what you want to accomplish and expect results. Knowing exactly what you want is how to get exactly what you want. If you are unsure of what you want in life, your expectations should be low. Controlling your destiny starts with knowing yourself and what you want to accomplish. Create goals that are structured in a way that is very specific, declaring that you are going to do something, that it will happen over a certain timeframe, and that it will be in a particular amount.

Create goals that are Measurable. Having measurable goals allows you to better review the progress you have made. This type of goal has two major measurable milestones: a dollar amount and time. Within a set timeframe you will pay a particular amount into your debt. There are very specific and measurable milestones within this goal. You can revisit the goal halfway through the set timeframe and review how much you paid into your debt up to that time. If you are on track, there would be around half the amount paid and remaining in the loan. If this is not the case, then review how to get back on track and, if that seems unlikely, make a decision on modifying the goal and milestones. For longer goals, I recommend revisiting the goals every quarter of the way through and determine if you are 25% closer to your goal than before.

<u>Ascertain if the goal is Attainable.</u> The more accurate you are in this step, the greater the likelihood your goals will not need to be modified in the future. It can be difficult to judge whether or not the goal is attainable. There is nothing wrong with being aggressive with your goals but you need to be realistic given your current situation as discussed in *Financial Assessment and Strategy Building.* Do not doubt what you can achieve. However, make sure the goals are practical when considering available resources. For example, let's say you were to set a goal to pay off your debt in the next month, and your total debt is more money than what you possess, or will possess at the end of the month. It is highly unlikely that you will achieve the goal, and you have set yourself up for failure. Having goals that are unattainable can cause loss of confidence when you fail to accomplish them and you may give up. Know your limits and your financial situation, and create goals accordingly.

<u>Relevant goals are key.</u> The best way to determine relevance is to ask yourself why you are focusing on this goal and what achieving it means to

you. These are important questions to answer, and need to be carefully considered. During the initial phase of writing down your goals, you may have written goals that are no longer relevant to the ultimate goal of becoming debt-free. Determining if the goal is relevant or not will help you to prioritize the goals that you should be focusing on now and remove those that are less important.

Determine if these goals are Timely. Deadlines are a necessity when it comes to setting goals. It is easy to become complacent when goals are open-ended. When goals are time-based it adds a level of urgency and encourages discipline. The deadlines set for each goal need to be realistic and achievable.

At this point, you should now have goals that are thorough and that are written in a manner that gives you confidence that they can be achieved. However, you still have not determined where to begin. This can be achieved by adopting the "one thing" approach for each goal.

The one-thing approach can work on either milestones or goals. It breaks it down and provides the basis of where to begin. First, start by looking at the overall goal; for example, "pay all debts off within five years." You now want to break that down even further. Ask yourself "What is the one thing I can do this year that will get me closer to my goal?" After that is determined, continue to break it down into manageable pieces: What can be done in the next six months? What can be done in the next three months? What can be done this month? Take the time to think about each one of these questions and be truthful with yourself. There is always one thing you can be doing that will help you progress through your debt-free journey. The answer to these questions could be as simple as making your payments on time, or paying a little extra into your debt. Every day is an opportunity to take one step closer to achieving your goals. In the case of debt, the seemingly small purchases made on a daily basis make a large impact when accumulated over time. There are many daily opportunities to save money, such as making coffee at home rather than stopping at a coffee shop, or packing a lunch instead of buying. You will be amazed at the amount of money that can be saved by taking a day-by-day approach, and staying disciplined with every purchase made. I encourage you to experiment for a week, replace at least one of your daily expenses with a substitute from home, and track the savings. You will see first-hand how these seemingly menial purchases add up to significant savings. The goals must be taken seriously and you need to do whatever is necessary in order to accomplish them, even if that requires sacrifice. Once your goals are met and you are debt-free, you can return to spending money on niceties like coffee and lunches out, but for now that money will have a greater impact when put toward becoming debt-free.

There are many ways that you can increase your likelihood of being successful with your goals. In addition to writing them down on a piece of paper, a proven method has been to make copies, and set them around the places that you frequent the most. This may be next to your bathroom mirror, next to your computer screen, or on your refrigerator. Seeing your goals often will ensure they stay on your mind, and this will trigger you to stay disciplined. Saying your goals out loud will have a major impact on your success as well. Tell your family and friends about your goals and what you are planning. When you take this approach, you become accountable and hopefully your loved ones will do their best to support you, and help to keep you on track if you stumble.

Your goals and milestones do not have to be fixed either. You absolutely need to commit, and do not want to keep changing your goals and milestones. However, there will be times when a goal or milestone either can no longer be achieved or life circumstances occur, and it needs to be pushed back. When this happens, be flexible. Review your goal or milestone and determine if there is a different approach that can be taken, or rewrite them in a manner that makes sense for your circumstances.

Now your goals and milestones are well defined, and you have a granular view of what you are going to accomplish as you work your way through your journey to become debt-free. You should feel good about your goals and milestones, and be motivated to start working toward them.

Chapter Exercises

1. What is your *why*?

_____

_____

_____

_____

2. Write each of your goals in the **S.M.A.R.T.** format along with their milestones.

_____

_____

_____

_____

_____

_____

_____

Becoming Debt-Free

Getting to this phase is a major milestone. Your mindset is aligned with your goals and you have developed mental exercises that will keep you focused. A strategy and plan of action has been established to guide your journey to becoming debt-free. Through the planning process, you developed a solid understanding of your current finances as well as all the details around your debt. You have defined goals in a way that they will give you the best opportunity to be successful and you know exactly what you want to achieve. You should feel confident and excited to begin to conquer your debt. If you have any doubts, return to the sections that you are unsure about and repeat those processes. It is important that you are confident in every area before continuing. To get clarity on any piece of this process you are unsure of, visit www.thedebtfreeme.com. You will find all the tools, formulas, and information discussed in the previous chapters.

It is time to test yourself and your discipline. There are no easy ways out of debt; no one else is going to pay your debt for you and make all your financial troubles disappear. This is a day-to-day effort that will require patience and fortitude. In times of turmoil, adjust your mindset and power through.

Your debt is only temporary; it does not define you and it will be paid off eventually. Anything worth having is worth fighting for, so return to your *why*, believe in yourself, and work hard to pay down your debts.

In times when you feel you are not making progress, revisit your timeline to see your actual progress and get an idea of what is coming next. Since maintaining focus is paramount, your timeline provides a clear picture of where your focus needs to be. I lived off my timeline and when I was feeling like my debt was overwhelming and I wanted to give up, I reviewed my timeline to check my progress. Seeing the progress I had made and how my hard work was paying off was incredibly uplifting to my mental state, and it gave me the boost I needed to adjust my mindset to stay disciplined.

Your goals should be relatively fixed, but your plan and strategy should be fluid. As you begin your journey, things will change, mostly for the good. During the course of paying off debt, there will be changes to the key metrics on which you based your planning and strategy. When the loan balances decrease, so will the interest that is being accumulated. This is important to consider if you are basing your strategy on interest (Avalanche and Hybrid methods). More important than reassessing the

plan and strategy, is reassessing your finances. While
you may be reaching your initial goals, you may
discover you were too conservative during the initial
planning phase. Reassessing your finances will
determine if there is additional money that could be
put toward your debt. If there is, make the adjustments
to your spreadsheets and enter that excess amount into
the additional payment category. You will see how this
increase to the total amount paid into your debt each
month positively affects your overall timeline. This
reassessment will also help to account for any missed
or spikes in variable expenses. A water bill, for
example, can be this type of expense. These expenses
are not always billed on a monthly basis, they could
be billed every 45 days or every other month.
Therefore, the surplus you have to put toward your
debt as an additional payment may fluctuate. Be
mindful of these expenses, and plan accordingly to
maximize your payments during these fluctuations.
Watch for trends and use caution when spending
money you believe is "extra". It is best to wait a
month or so to be certain it truly is extra. It is also
important to take into account expenses that occur
longer-term, such as: car insurance, home insurance,
life insurance policies, etc. For those expenses,
determine how much you will need to save each

month to cover these and add a section for them in your spreadsheet.

Throughout the journey, you may become careless with your finances and begin to spend money on things that are not necessary. Because of these instances, it is even more important to reassess your finances regularly. Regularly reassessing will provide an outlook on how you are spending your money. Return to the early stages of the planning phase and dive deep into the spending of every dollar. This process will give insight into any expenses you may have not realized were causing an issue. This provides the opportunity to realign your goals and make sure you are making as much progress as possible given your resources.

While the execution phase will test your patience and discipline, try to have fun during this process. Every paycheck should be seen as an opportunity. It is an opportunity to get closer to your goals. You may already be excited on payday, but try to channel that excitement toward the opportunity to put another payment into your debt. I had a unique way of looking at my debt: I used my imagination and envisioned this journey as a game. I would imagine I was being chased by a monster, and the only weapon against the monster was a ball of fire. As I ran away from the monster, I would throw fire at him. Each ball of fire would shrink the monster little by little until he was eventually destroyed. In this game, the monster was my mountain of debt and the balls of fire were the money being paid into my loans. Using my imagination and making a game of the situation helped to keep me focused. I would get excited every payday to be that much closer to overcoming my monster. Eventually, the payment on payday will achieve a milestone, and that is an exciting moment in your timeline as you are now one step closer to being debt-free. This excitement is the main reason why you create milestones early in the process. These steps help guide you and provide confidence that you are moving in the right direction. When the amount of debt is large, paying down the smaller loans may not feel like a major victory, but it is. Be excited for each loan paid off regardless of the amount. With each and every payoff, you reduce accruing interest, and that is cause for celebration.

You are saving money. Whether it feels that way or not, every payment toward debt is actually *saving* money. Every single payment regardless of how much, is decreasing the amount of interest that will be accumulated. It may seem like there is no difference when you make these payments, but there is. Over time, you will save hundreds or thousands of dollars depending on your timeline and the life of your debt. The savings from each payment made allows you to put that money into the loans you are targeting in your strategy and will begin to contribute to principal-heavy payments. For me, every loan was different but, on average, my monthly interest total would decrease by nearly $20 a month. Which was roughly $240 saved each year per loan. Although that may not seem like a lot per year, it can be thousands saved over the entire lifespan of your debts.

Sticking to your plan and making your regular payments is a win. Even if these occurrences are happening every week or so. Whenever you have an instance that requires any amount of discipline, it is important that you appreciate those moments. Being disciplined is not easy and is an attribute that many may struggle with. Be proud of your achievements, really take them in, as this will motivate you to continue to be disciplined.

The debt-free journey will test your willpower and your discipline. It is very important that you do not let it wear you down or cause unneeded stress. You need to live your life while maintaining discipline and working toward your goals. This is not always an easy thing to balance. It will take compromise and sacrifice. However, it can be done with careful consideration and thought behind what living your life means to you.

There are many online resources and books on how people have worked hard to make extra money or cut corners in order to pay down their debt faster. While this is a fine approach, it is not an approach that will work for everyone. Working another job, or overtime at your current job, could be detrimental to your mental health as well as to the relationships in your life. I applaud those who are able to do these things and complete their goals sooner by working harder to put more money toward their debt. However, for me this was not something I was interested in. I knew it was going to take time to pay down my debt. I could have worked another job to pay my debt off a year or so earlier, but that was not appealing to me. The time spent with my family is more valuable to me than the amount of money I could make at another job. With the time I have before and after work I am able to have breakfast, dinner, and spend time with my family. Had I chosen to work another job, I would have to eliminate one, if not all of these. By deciding to build a strategy based on my current financial situation, rather than taking on another job to increase my income, my mood has been positive overall as I am not as stressed or wearing myself down. This approach is not meant to deter you from doing whatever you can to pay your debt off sooner. Do whatever you can if you have the fortitude to squeeze as much money as you can from your spare time and current financial situation. In moments of feeling burnt out, cut back and take time to enjoy yourself. Everyone is different and what works for some may not work for others. To truly find success, maintain your sanity throughout this process, avoid burning out, and implement a sustainable approach to life that fosters success.

Do not compare your financial situation to other people during your journey. It can be easy to get depressed when you see that someone paid their debts off sooner than you, or if someone did not have debt at all. When having these thoughts, return to your mindset exercises and realign your focus on *your* current situation. Focus only on the things that you can control. It is likely that the other people are not in the exact same situation as you. They may have had less debt to begin with, they may make more money, or have less expenses and are able to put more toward their debt. Comparing yourself to others who have achieved their financial goals before you can lead to negative thoughts or feelings. However, I encourage you to compare your strategies and techniques to those who have been successful in accomplishing goals similar to yours. There is a lot to be learned from other people's strategies and techniques. When reviewing other approaches, determine if there are components of their strategy that have been more successful than yours and implement what worked for them into your own.

You may be faced with challenges and obstacles you will be forced to overcome during your journey. During my journey, my manager came to me one day with some unexpected news: I had been laid off. I was terrified because I was not sure how I would pay my loan minimums while I was unemployed. With the paychecks I received before my last day, I decided to take the money I was putting as an **Additional Payment** against my loans and put it toward my emergency fund. Because of my financial assessment, I had a thorough understanding of my finances. I knew that with my emergency fund and my savings, I did not have to worry about how I would pay my loan minimums for a few months. This emphasizes the importance of having a complete understanding of your current financial situation. Putting everything into my spreadsheet and carefully reviewing all aspects of my finances meant I was prepared for this curveball and could easily adapt. Taking this approach gave me peace of mind, as it bought me time and allowed me to focus my energy on getting a new job. If you find yourself in this situation, and months pass and you are still unemployed, you will need to review the terms of your loans and see what your options are. Your loan provider may offer options for delaying payments such as putting your loans in a Deferment or Forbearance status.

Through these times of hardship, it is also important to leverage a support system if possible. Leverage any support system you can through these times. Lean on any family or friends if you can until you are able to get back on your feet and get your life in order. Keep your end goals in mind and do whatever is necessary not to detract from them. Remember that your mentality is everything, and it will be your mentality that gets you through this hardship. Reflect on the progress you have made towards your goals this far and remind yourself that this is only a temporary setback, and that you will overcome it.

Once you have put in all the time and work necessary to accomplish what you set out to achieve, and you are debt-free, celebrate! To be debt-free is a major accomplishment. Being debt-free is a weight lifted off your shoulders and can feel like a new beginning. Take time to celebrate and enjoy being debt-free. But, be sure not to get complacent. Do not let go of the reins too much and accumulate debt again. Go back to the beginning, and start over with different goals. You have built a skillset and understanding of finances that is far superior to many others. Do not waste this skillset; put this discipline to use. Act like the money you were previously putting into your student loan debt does not exist, and put this money toward something else. Focus it toward any other debts you may have and if you do not have any other debts, put it into your savings or retirement. The tools you will possess once you get through this journey of becoming debt-free will be beneficial in your life and will give you confidence in your ability to accomplish your financial goals. These principles and practices are not limited to student loan debt; they apply to all financial goals. Do not let all the hard work you have put in go to waste. You now have all the tools needed to be successful and to become debt-free.

Chapter Exercises

1. How frequently will you review your plan and strategy? Set a reminder.

_____

_____

_____

_____

_____

2. How often will you review your expenses? Set a reminder.

_____

_____

_____

_____

_____

3. Are you living a sustainable lifestyle while making your debt payments on your set schedule? If not, what is getting in the way?

_____

_____

_____

_____

_____

4. Are you currently working more than one job? If so, is it absolutely necessary in order to meet your goals or can you instead further eliminate expenses?

_____

_____

_____

_____

_____

5. How is your outlook on debt? How confident are you in reaching your goals?

_____

_____

_____

_____

_____

_____

Appendix A

Overview of Completed Spreadsheet

Income	
Yearly	$60,000.00
Monthly	$3,742.78
Paychecks	$1,871.39

Fixed Expenses	
Total Monthly Payment	$197.14
Car Payment	$200.00
Spotify	$10.00
Gym	$20.00
Cell phone	$60.00
Rent	$900.00
Internet	$40.00
Total	**$1,427.14**

Variable Expenses	
Gas	$90.00
Groceries	$400.00
Restaurants and Entertainment	$100.00
Water	$40.00
Electric	$80.00
Total	**$710.00**

Emergency Fund	$600.00

Monthly Net Income	$3,742.78
Fixed Expenses Total	$1,427.14
Variable Expenses Total	$710.00
Disposable Income	$1,605.64

Additional Debt Payment	

Current Date	1/1/2020
Total Debt	$20,450.01
Average Interest Rate	5.85%
Total Monthly Interest	$106.30
Total Yearly Interest	$1,275.62
Months to Debt-Free	145
Debt-Free Date	1/1/2032

Appendix B

Calculation for Disposable Income

Figure 1 represents the completed Disposable Income overview

Figure 2 shows the formulas to calculate Disposable Income

Figure 1

Monthly Net Income	$3,742.78
Fixed Expenses Total	$1,427.14
Variable Expenses Total	$710.00
Disposable Income	$1,605.64

Figure 2

	F	G	H
4	Monthly Net Income		=D4
5	Fixed Expenses Total		=D15
6	Variable Expenses Total		=D23
7			
8	Disposable Income		=H4-H5-H6

H4 = Monthly Net Income (D4 = Monthly from Income Category (Figure 3))

H5 = Fixed Expenses (D15 = Total from Fixed Expenses Category (Figure 3))

H6 = Variable Expenses Total (D23 = Total from Variable Expenses Category (Figure 3))

Figure 3

	B	C	D
2	**Income**		
3	Yearly		$60,000.00
4	Monthly		$3,742.78
5	Paychecks		$1,871.39
6			
7	**Fixed Expenses**		
8	Total Monthly Payment		$197.14
9	Car Payment		$200.00
10	Spotify		$10.00
11	Gym		$20.00
12	Cell phone		$60.00
13	Rent		$900.00
14	Internet		$40.00
15	**Total**		**$1,427.14**
16			
17	**Variable Expenses**		
18	Gas		$90.00
19	Groceries		$400.00
20	Restaurants and Entertainment		$100.00
21	Water		$40.00
22	Electric		$80.00
23	**Total**		**$710.00**

Appendix C

Overview of Debt

Figure 1 represents the completed view of all debt.
Figure 2 shows how to calculate Yearly Interest (Loan
Balance x Interest Rate)
Figure 3 shows how to calculate Monthly Interest
(Yearly Interest Divided by 12)

Figure 1.

Unique Identifier	Monthly Minimum	Loans: Balance	Interest rate	Monthly Interest	Yearly Interest
1	$19.17	$3,418.72	6.80%	$19.37	$232.47
2	$88.79	$7,834.83	6.80%	$44.40	$532.77
A	$74.28	$6,568.15	6.41%	$35.08	$421.02
B	$14.89	$2,628.31	3.40%	$7.45	$89.36
Totals	$197.14	$20,450.01	5.85%	$106.30	$1,275.62

Figure 2.

	F	G	H	I	J	K
20	Unique Identifier	Monthly Minimum	Loans: Balance	Interest rate	Monthly Interest	Yearly Interest
21	1	$19.17	$3,418.72	6.80%	$19.37	=(H21*I21)
22	2	$88.79	$7,834.83	6.80%	$44.40	$532.77
23	A	$74.28	$6,568.15	6.41%	$35.08	$421.02
24	B	$14.89	$2,628.31	3.40%	$7.45	$89.36
25	Totals	$197.14	820,450.01	5.85%	$106.30	$1,275.62

Figure 3.

	F	G	H	I	J	K
20	Unique Identifier	Monthly Minimum	Loans: Balance	Interest rate	Monthly Interest	Yearly Interest
21	1	$19.17	$3,418.72	6.80%	=(K21)/12	$232.47
22	2	$88.79	$7,834.83	6.80%	$44.40	$532.77
23	A	$74.28	$6,568.15	6.41%	$35.08	$421.02
24	B	$14.89	$2,628.31	3.40%	$7.45	$89.36
25	Totals	$197.14	$20,450.01	5.85%	$106.30	$1,275.62

Appendix D

Formulas for Months to Debt-Free and Debt-Free Date

Figure 1 shows the calculation for Months to Debt-Free

Figure 2 shows the calculation to Debt-Free Date

Figure 1.

Additional Debt Payment	$1,605.64

Current Date	1/1/2020
Total Debt	$20,450.01
Average Interest Rate	5.85%
Total Monthly Interest	$106.30
Total Yearly Interest	$1,275.62
Months to Debt-Free	=NPER(G14/12,-D8,G13)
Debt-Free Date	12/1/2020

G14 = average monthly interest rate
D8 = total monthly payment
G13 = total current balance

Figure 2.

Additional Debt Payment	$1,605.64

Current Date	1/1/2020
Total Debt	$20,450.01
Average Interest Rate	5.85%
Total Monthly Interest	$106.30
Total Yearly Interest	$1,275.62
Months to Debt-Free	12
Debt-Free Date	? =EDATE(G12,G17)

G12 = current date
G17 = Months to Debt-Free

Appendix E

Sorting Debt Data

Figure 1 shows how to sort the debt data

Figure 2 shows how the data will look once sorted

Figure 1.

Column J represents the Monthly Interest

Sorting Z to A will sort from highest interest to lowest interest.

Figure 2.

F	G	H	I	J	K
Unique Identifier	**Monthly Minimum**	**Loans: Balance**	**Interest rate**	**Monthly Interest**	**Yearly Interest**
2	$88.79	$7,834.83	6.80%	$44.40	$532.77
A	$74.28	$6,568.15	6.41%	$35.08	$421.02
1	$19.17	$3,418.72	6.80%	$19.37	$232.47
B	$14.89	$2,628.31	3.40%	$7.45	$89.36
Totals	**$197.14**	**$20,450.01**	**5.85%**	**$106.30**	**$1,275.62**

Appendix F

Overview of How to Calculate for Total Monthly Payment

Figure 1 shows the calculation for Total Monthly Payment

Figure 1.

Fixed Expenses	
Total Monthly Payment	$1,802.78
Car Payment	$200.00
Spotify	$10.00
Gym	$20.00
Cell phone	$60.00
Rent	$900.00
Internet	$40.00
Total	**$3,032.78**

H10 = Additional Debt Payment (Figure 2)
G25 = Total Monthly Minimums (Figure 3)

Figure 2.

	F	G	H
10	Additional Debt Payment		$1,515.64

Figure 3.

	F	G	H	I	J	K
20	Unique Identifier	Monthly Minimum	Loans: Balance	Interest rate	Monthly Interest	Yearly Interest
21	1	$19.17	$3,418.72	6.80%	$19.37	$232.47
22	2	$88.79	$7,834.83	6.80%	$44.40	$532.77
23	A	$74.28	$6,568.15	6.41%	$35.08	$421.02
24	B	$14.89	$2,628.31	3.40%	$7.45	$89.36
25	Totals	$197.14	$20,450.01	5.85%	$106.30	$1,275.62

Appendix G

Overview and Formulas for the Amortization Chart

In Figure 1, the Additional Debt Payment value can be modified to show how these additional payments will affect your timeline

Figure 2 shows the formulas used to create the amortization chart

Figure 1.

Total Debt	$20,450.01
Average Interest Rate	5.85%
Monthly Debt Minimums	$197.14
Additional Debt Payment	$1,515.64
Total Debt Payment	$1,712.78

Months	Date	Interest Gained/Month	Payment to Principal	Balance
1	1/1/2020	-$99.74	$1,613.04	$18,836.97
2	2/1/2020	-$91.87	$1,620.91	$17,216.06
3	3/1/2020	-$83.96	$1,628.81	$15,587.24
4	4/1/2020	-$76.02	$1,636.76	$13,950.49
5	5/1/2020	-$68.04	$1,644.74	$12,305.75
6	6/1/2020	-$60.02	$1,652.76	$10,652.98
7	7/1/2020	-$51.96	$1,660.82	$8,992.16
8	8/1/2020	-$43.86	$1,668.92	$7,323.24
9	9/1/2020	-$35.72	$1,677.06	$5,646.17
10	10/1/2020	-$27.54	$1,685.24	$3,960.93
11	11/1/2020	-$19.32	$1,693.46	$2,267.47
12	12/1/2020	-$11.06	$1,701.72	$565.75
13	1/1/2021	-$2.76	$1,710.02	-$1,144.27

Figure 2.

Total Debt	=Finances!H13
Average Interest Rate	=Finances!I25
Monthly Debt Minimums	=Finances!G25
Additional Debt Payment	$1,515.64
Total Debt Payment	=D4+D5

Months	Date	Interest Gained/Month	Payment to Principal	Balance
1	=Finances!H12	=IPMT($D$3,1,B9,D2)/12	=$D$6+D9	=D2-E9
=B9+1	=EDATE(C9,1)	=IPMT($D$3,1,B10,F9)/12	=$D$6+D10	=F9-E10
=B10+1	=EDATE(C10,1)	=IPMT($D$3,1,B11,F10)/12	=$D$6+D11	=F10-E11
=B11+1	=EDATE(C11,1)	=IPMT($D$3,1,B12,F11)/12	=$D$6+D12	=F11-E12
=B12+1	=EDATE(C12,1)	=IPMT($D$3,1,B13,F12)/12	=$D$6+D13	=F12-E13
=B13+1	=EDATE(C13,1)	=IPMT($D$3,1,B14,F13)/12	=$D$6+D14	=F13-E14
=B14+1	=EDATE(C14,1)	=IPMT($D$3,1,B15,F14)/12	=$D$6+D15	=F14-E15
=B15+1	=EDATE(C15,1)	=IPMT($D$3,1,B16,F15)/12	=$D$6+D16	=F15-E16
=B16+1	=EDATE(C16,1)	=IPMT($D$3,1,B17,F16)/12	=$D$6+D17	=F16-E17
=B17+1	=EDATE(C17,1)	=IPMT($D$3,1,B18,F17)/12	=$D$6+D18	=F17-E18
=B18+1	=EDATE(C18,1)	=IPMT($D$3,1,B19,F18)/12	=$D$6+D19	=F18-E19
=B19+1	=EDATE(C19,1)	=IPMT($D$3,1,B20,F19)/12	=$D$6+D20	=F19-E20
=B20+1	=EDATE(C20,1)	=IPMT($D$3,1,B21,F20)/12	=$D$6+D21	=F20-E21

Made in the USA
Middletown, DE
24 October 2020

22716412R00061